Some stuff
about me and you

Lee Richards

Presentation by *BookLeaf Publishing*

Web: www.bookleafpub.com

E-mail: info@bookleafpub.com

ISBN: 9789358368130

First edition 2023

For you, of course

PREFACE

In the letters we read to each other at our wedding, I told you that I didn't want to reference any of the media I so often talked about, because I wanted the words to be entirely my own. I wanted on that day to express to you the almost *a priority* of my love for you. That was the right choice for that day.

Today, in acknowledgement of how much I am the product of my world, I hold myself to no such standard. Much of what's here is me, obscure and arcane with *a posteriority*. (As an example, that's Kant waving at you through my relationship to your baby brother, Lampe in tow.) (No wampas yet, though. They'll show up later. Also, he lost his arm, so it's pretty impressive he's waving at you through the nerdy friends we share.) (This third set of parentheses is me being annoying. You can decide which of our relations is waving at you from here.) The world is a context for understanding. You are a context for my understanding. There is no I without the we. Many of the allusions in here make me laugh, or inspire me, or bring me joy. Many we have shared and discussed, and those discussions, even more, inspire, make me laugh,

bring me joy. I think you feel the same. So this is
me, me now, in context, writing to you.

To Start

It's been about ten years since you said to me,
"Wanna watch Game of Thrones?"
And I sat next to you
Closer than usual,
And you said to me
"Hey."

And the dragon of desire,
Long suppressed and repressed,
Buried under my hoard
Of incense,
Of self-justification,
Of desolate-fear,
Woke.

Falling Water

We drove for hours,
Four hours,
To see the waterfall.
It was raining when we left.
I was almost out of money and well on my way
to failing out.

I wanted to impress you
And hide,
And you saw the failing and falling,
And you saw the spark of creation in the rain,
And you saw back a decade
Through working and grease and God's spell
To wind in the tree.
And I think somehow you saw ahead
To building and chopping and growing,
And you

Paid for pizza in Canada.

The Weight

Let's stay maudlin a little longer.

This is all of
Me, after all.
And of me all
Is a lot.

A New Religion

In The Midge,
I don't think I realized how unhealthy it was, that
Salubrious lake-air, that
Incense of living two lives.
I was home,
Sort of home;
You were only two hours away.
But still I sought home in candlelight,
Ever resenting bread and wine but hungry,
Ever craving bread and cheese,
In things passed away.
Why do you seek the living among the dead?

I already had it, not manna at all,
And the mud was not washed from my eyes,
And the plank was still in my eye,
And the stone was still in my hand,
Because I still tried to consume the new light.
If I leave this unhappy place, where will my
Eden be? Thou fool.

There is no I without the We.
Divine love is grace,
That we need not change to be perfect and we
are called to change.

That perfect must synthesize the world
And the self's desires for the self
Like Eidolons.
I love you, you're perfect, now change.
Truth is I love you.

There is no I without the We.
We choose to love and be loved.

These
Don't knock around in golden cages. These
Won't be hidden and alone. These
Can't be held in the cup, and they
Require no licking of the floor.
They need no raiment.

I needed no priest.
I needed my partner.
There are guides
Who occupy the quieter coves of the spirit,
Pointing the way out.

My Heart in the Highlands

When did you know?
You tell me always.

You always knew your heart was not your own?
That
It lives outside your body?

My heart is not here.

It's a-chasing itself. It is in the world. In the
Highlands, in the North.
Wherever you go I will go
Bidding farewell and carrying its marks and
scars as witness.
This ancient knowledge you knew all along
Etched in your bones and sending from you like
sunlight.
Yes, there is valor where there is love.

And you, flesh of my flesh,
You too lead and you too follow,
And so together we press on.

Reunification

Before I could ask you to marry me,
You laid bare to me your insecurity
Which you often push to the deep shadows
From me and the world and I think yourself.

I hesitate to call that the honest you,
The secret soul that tries to stand alone,
But a black and dense part
That I also love
Though I see myself reflected there.

Long do I look there because
I am comforted seeing the anticipating I before
the we,
That we are together in time and
After the dazzle of day is done
Only the dark, dark night
Shows to my eyes the stars.

Five Rings

The first ring was an old thing
From Luther long ago,
Pulled from my hand sat on the sand
In ocean's ebb and flow.

The second ring you, kind to bring,
Bought at the resort stall
Twisting and glyphed, Poseidon did lift
With his lake this time - what gall!

With third then avoiding the water, annoyed in
Good reason, I got rubber black
And though I'm not sure, lost on Schwan's truck
with cured
Hams and ice creams and a job that I do not
want back.

The fourth one is yours, in your jewelry drawers
Just outgrown so with smaller replaced
By identical one ordered from Amazon
With wood and star stuff and much to my taste.

So fifth, finger-borne, even now by me worn
Is this promise, this sign metal casted,
To let the world know that however we grow
And whatever we lose, our love lasted.

(Verse, oy.)

Three Sizes

I didn't ever live on a snowy mountaintop
So I don't think I ever got the hint
That my heart was in need of growing.

But then you showed me three pregnancy tests
With three plus signs
(Or was it three double lines?
The memory is the feeling.)
We three were together.
The rest I forget.

And my life became Christmas morning,
And our Rose
Bloomed.

And I watched you lie unclothed with her.
The sleepers are very beautiful.
And as you slept I also held her;
And at three in the morning
My heart grew as she cried and I
Kissed that head full of hair.

Three months after
that night that my heart grew
We were shocked,
stunned,
exhausted,
worried, and
positive again.

Tired, the year came new,
And our Miles
Moved us forward.

And I watched you lie unclothed with him.
The sleepers are very beautiful
As they lie.
And as you slept I also held him;
As an answer to a craving only my heart knew
he pressed his face with your eyes
Into my chest
Where my heart grew and I
Was made anew in love again.

Three more years
The four of us had to complete our team;
In the throes of pandemic and the dumpster fire
We were creation.

The flowers grew in spring,
Though all around was the stink of the fear of
death and the unknown,
And our Shaw
Sprung a spud from the earth.

And I watched you lie unclothed with him.
The sleepers are very beautiful
As they lie
As they lie.
And as you slept I also held him;
Laying together by the hearth, he smiled
And it was a smile radiant and gripping and for
me,
Making my heart grow a third time.

Three sizes larger,
Never a Grinch but never before more who I am
Than I am now,
A heart already outside now swelled, matured,
And changed
Ever changed
In the magic of three.

Your Smile

Can we look back?
I was thirteen when you first smiled at me, and
you were twelve
Or maybe fourteen and thirteen.
The memory is a fog that your face cuts through
With sunlight and starlight
And I thought, "Oh, pretty,"
Not knowing that one day I would live for that
smile,
Ache and act to see you happy,
Change and build and lose and grow
All to bask in the radiance
That lights my way and lays me down.

I was twenty-seven when you said "Hey,"
And when you eased away
And my lips were wet and my arms tingled
You smiled
And your smile was pleasure and triumph and
fate
And kindness.

And the deed to my life had a new signature,
And my heart moved out of my body,
And a smile I was too much a coward, too much
embarrassed,
To accept a decade earlier
Now had me because I didn't know why.

That smile, your smile, was for me.

Your Body

Your body
Your body
My brain stops
I wrote the title first and now there are no words.

Your Brain

I want my brain to interface with your brain.
I want to marvel at the speed, the creativity,
the ever-humming din of being Annie.

What songs flying free,
What visionary structures,
Could I know suffused in you?

What love, what care,
Uncompromising and reasoned,
Still always exuding and finding
We who need?

There is no post within you,
No day without you,
Where I could ever wish to be,
That then I scorn to change my state with kings.

Because you, all of you,
I reverence and delight in,
But most your vigorous and expanded mind.

Your Hands

See that a person is righteous because of her
works, not her faith.
You are you in the world.
Healing the world is not for you a beetle in a
box.

Just as you are the invention of me,
Your hands move your mind and your heart
And so you become the world
And the world becomes better.

Your work is your commitment to
Pioneer the movement of improvement
Through the boldness of science that
Measures and adapts and reasons and changes.

You risk when you move your heart out of your
body
To touch mine;
But you, fighter hero,
Move your beliefs, expose your action to
reaction,
Test your hopes against all opposition
Especially and always that which comes from
within.

Let us watch how you look;
Let us watch how you sculpt;
Let us watch how you rise,
Because with your hands you do not just work.

With your hands you hope.

Dammit, Walt

Annie, I'm trying to write love poetry. Like, this
is actually a thing I'm doing. I want to impress
you without hiding. But this format bounds a
boundless thing, right? Isn't the thesis of this
project that my love for you grows because we
share it as we live in the world?

The leaf of grass is no less than the journeywork
of the stars. The leaf of paper is time frozen,
accomplish'd and enclosing.

Because I am a born and bred Minnesotan, this
is my apology for writing a book of poetry to
you and for you and about you through me.

Ope.

Your Song

With your hands you hope
So in rising we rise
Yoked to you we sing ourselves in the world
And the eidolons we dream
Are our own each and shared
Brought nearer hearing your strains reecho
As we never walk alone

Star Trek

Huch 'oH ghu'vam neH lughajlu"a'?
tlhiHvaD HeS 'arqon'a'?
Qo'!
Do'Ha' je Say'moHwI'pu', tlhoblIj rurchugh,
yIghoS!
yIlopchu' 'ej qeylIS qa'
jIHvaD loDhomvam qelpu'!
tlhIngan lunuDbe' tlhIngan
DaH mIghqu' chargh!
bIQ'a'meyDaj
'ej ramjepvaD neH bIjatlh!"
tugh naQ yISIQ.
ngaQmo' tlhIvqu' rur,
tlhInganpu'wI' tlhIngan.

Is this all too much?
Has it gotten excessive or embarrassing?
No!
Like your song and your hands,
Let us be brave!
Let us have the courage to be vulnerable!
If we are to be damned, let us be damned for
who we really are!
The Klingon does not hide from her emotion,
Nor hide her emotion!

Passion lives in risk,
And the flux of time is not for the timid!
So let us write poems!
Because all poetry, even and especially
Shakespeare, belongs
In its original Klingon!

Versus

But let us also take stock of where we are
When in roughness,
Because the bold are not bold if they
Only expose their best angles.

Our communication hits and misses.
We hide ourselves from each other
And I let fester those things that need to be
addressed
And you know and you do.
I do little and expect great praise,
I am privileged and filthy,
I argue to argue,
I am insecure
And I blame the external for my behavior.

We are imperfect parents.
I discipline too hard;
I am inconsistent with limits;
I undermine you by being lazy when
You need me to work harder.

And you drive me to upset
When you overcorrect
Or you change without telling me
Or you don't see the difference between desired
and best
Or you cannot meet my desire with desire.

And sometimes our failings overwhelm our
good sense,
And sometimes our failings are papered over
Or addressed poorly,
And sometimes our failings lead to more
failings,
And we go to bed angry and dream angry and
wake angry.

We justify, justify.

I am imperfect, and I am not someone to fall
back on.
But in the morning we wake to try and to
Continue,

We make the choice.

Gilmore Girls

So who do you identify with most now?
If it's already Emily and you're only 37 (happy
birthday!), where do you grow?
Maybe you move on to Sookie next, embracing
your good taste with growing epicureanism?
Maybe you tilt into Paris, driven and hungry to
build a Babel of Behavior ever higher?
Could you regress, when Rosie can't choose
between Harvard or Yale?
Will you go nuts and become Babette while I
take up jazz piano?

Maybe it's a different show entirely?
Maybe you are becoming CJ?
Maybe I should get you a goldfish?

Why predict? And why pigeonhole? Can anyone
love a fantasy?
And would I ever stop choosing to love you?
Haven't you made every day better? Made me
feel rich as Logan, handsome as Dean, capable
as Jess?
And in finding myself reflected in these
fantasies, haven't I synthesized a better reality?
Harvested and grafted and grown?

So, what character, drawn to a use, flattened and
restricted in lines and two-dimensions, can you
become? Aren't you already infinitely more?
Do you identify with them, or do they, lucky
them, reflect some small facet of a woman
whole?

Oh no, is this a question poem?

I guess so.

Chat GPT

The robots might be taking over soon,
So I checked how these tubes would do if
They wrote a sonnet about my wife.
Here are the results:

Oh, my sweet wife, my heart's truest desire,
Your presence fill my days with boundless joy,
With each passing moment, my love grows
higher,
Like a flower that blooms without alloy.
Your eyes, like pools of sapphire blue,
Reflect the light of heaven's own grace,
And in your smile, I find a love so true,
That time nor distance could ever erase.
With every breath, I whisper your name,
And cherish the moments that we share,
For in your embrace, I am forever tame,
And the world outside simply disappears.
My dear wife, my love for you will never wane,
For you are the light that keeps me sane.

Not bad, right?
Maybe I should get a poetry implant.
It guessed wrong about your eyes, though.

Love in a Time of

What has COVID done to us?
I feel like we've adjusted our lives to
accommodate
Togetherness like we couldn't anticipate.
Days stretched to weeks as our family grew and
we were sardines, we five in this house with
twelve rooms.
And we grew in patience and understanding
As we did our best side by side
Looking forward
Or at each other when we could.
And in this odd pressure cooker,
I
fell harder.

We worked.
We made the choice to work.
Each day we had to make the choice again,
And each day we chose it.
To build and be built.
To change and be changed.
To adapt and let ourselves be adapted.
To trust and be trusted.
To love and be loved.
This strange new world was for me

Both a laboratory of vacuum-sealed family,
And a Bohemia with hearts on the windows.

And we faced it. Together we faced it.
Just as together we face each new challenge.
It won't be COVID again (hopefully),
And I don't know what comes next,
But I know we'll be together,
So the rest can be forgotten.

Togetherness that we can't anticipate
Is a We in the world.

Annie, I don't love you because I don't know
why. I love you because I choose to love you.
And so I shall through every season.

Candide

But
Could there be a poem that says life with you is
the best of all possible worlds?
Shouldn't that be a requirement of such a sappy
collection?
Or would it require an ironic denouement?

But
What about a poem that says life with you has
been imperfect?
Could I craft a couple of lines that in the end
would give you a sense of your perfection in
your imperfections and this imperfect
togetherness?

I've been trying since I met you.
I'm not John Legend.

Time Travel

Do you remember that feeling when we were
kids
During Halloween season
And we watched one of five channels
And there were commercials for Doritos or Kit
Kats
Or whatever and they were so spooky and
We got that clenched feeling that sucked our
shoulders into our stomachs
And it was so cool?

You weren't there yet, but

Do you remember learning to pray was just
asking God for the things you want and you
didn't have big dreams but you wanted the Twins
to win the Series because it was fun to stay up
late and cheer with Mom and Dad?

You weren't there yet, but

Do you remember the time of I before We,
When every battle felt blooded
And we tilted so hard at trying to destroy our
insecurities
While riding our bikes and learning to swear?

You had arrived and I was not ready for you yet,
but

Do you remember when we were on the
Godspell set and we were trying so hard to be
good actors and make real tears behind chain
link and produce beautiful music so that we
could pull other people's tears from their eyes?

We were together and I wasn't ready yet, but

Do you remember 3am talks,
Tethered to the wall so the miles were fewer,
Gossiping about our friends and trying to sound
Smart and cool and funny
And wanting so badly to be with you?

We were together but together eluded me and I
didn't know it but I needed you to be patient, and
I didn't know that was what I was asking for, but

Do you remember the house?
The House? Where we tried even harder and
everything slanted and our friends got mad at
you and you left and I didn't do anything
because I thought I was getting messages from
God through Deep Space Nine?

We were close and I thought myself so far away
and it hurts to see you with other guys because
I'm selfish and I want it both ways and I
convince myself you're not there, but

Do you remember sitting on white couches
getting dirty and waking me up and When Harry
Met Sally?

We were there and that was you then, but

Do you remember in Mexico, how you looked
so good, so prepossessing
In the sunrises over the ocean, and I watched the
iguanas and
You were annoyed that I had eyes that went
anywhere but on you,
And you wished we could be the fun table
Because we were committed now and facing the
future?

We were there and that was you then, but

Do you remember Christmas morning when we
watch the kids unwrap presents and suddenly we
are our parents and we get how it is to be tired
and happy and the purveyors of discovery in our
hope for years coming?

We are there, and that, to me, is you now, in a
moment perfect and needing to change, but

Do you remember arguments and forgivings as
they grow and become little I's of their own,
Graduations in the 2030s,
Weddings planned and imperfect, where we
have strong opinions on our kids' musical tastes,
Holding babies and remembering when the
babies were them,
Realizing that wisdom is the name of the path
we've walked
With still more miles to go?

You aren't there yet, but

Do you remember how I'll be in a hospital with
something stupid like cancer or Alzheimer's
And we'll be old and quiet and together
And we'll look best we can on lives with things
we're proud of and things we regret,
On our beautiful progeny and the work we did
and the things we built that others are already
changing
And feel at peace that in a few hundred years
we'll be forgotten
Because we are contented ordinary people doing
our best in a world that has been chopping and

growing and even sugar cake baked in a
cardboard box,
And in a few millennia our Facebook pages
might be data points in history books written by
ape robot spacepeople?

You aren't there yet, but

But somehow you are there,
The you who are you now,
And somehow you saw it when we met,
And somehow you saw it when the water was
falling and I was in twain,
And somehow you saw it when our songs were
sung by our friends and our family to our family
and our friends,
And somehow you saw it when we became three
and four and five,
That when we were and are and will still be
together
We are at an acme of things accomplish'd
Enclosing things to be.